BISON

Amy-Jane Beer

Grolier
an imprint of

■SCHOLASTIC

www.scholastic.com/librarypublishing

Published 2008 by Grolier
An imprint of Scholastic Library Publishing
Old Sherman Turnpike, Danbury,
Connecticut 06816

For The Brown Reference Group plc
Project Editor: Jolyon Goddard
Copy-editors: Lesley Ellis, Lisa Hughes,
    Wendy Horobin
Picture Researcher: Clare Newman
Designers: Jeni Child, Lynne Ross,
    Sarah Williams
Managing Editor: Bridget Giles

Volume ISBN-13: 978-0-7172-6249-6
Volume ISBN-10: 0-7172-6249-9

Nature's children. Set 2.
    p. cm.
  Includes bibliographical references and
  index.
  ISBN-13: 978-0-7172-8081-0
  ISBN-10: 0-7172-8081-0
  1. Animals--Encyclopedias, Juvenile. I.
  Grolier (Firm)
  QL49.N383 2007
  590--dc22
                        2007026928

Printed and bound in China

PICTURE CREDITS

Front Cover: **Shutterstock**: Michael J.
Thompson.

Back Cover: **Nature PL**: Ingo Arndt;
Shutterstock: Ronnie Howard, James E.
Knopf, Bartosz Wardzinski.

Corbis: Bettmann 41, Gunter Marx
Photography 34, Pierre Vauthey/Sygma 10;
FLPA: Mark Newman 18, 42; **Nature PL**:
Thomas Lazar 33; **Photolibrary.com**:
Melanie Acevedo 38, Richard Kettlewell 37;
Shutterstock: Sascha Burkard 22, Heather
L. Jones 2–3, 45, James E. Knopf 26–27, Willie
Linn 14, Jason Maehl 21, Todd Mestemacher
6, Vova Pomortzeff 13, Christian Riedel 17,
Marina Cano Trueba 30, TT Photo 5; **Still
Pictures**: R. Kaufung 9, R. Linke 46;
Supertock: Prisma 4, 29.

Contents

FACT FILE: Bison

Class	Mammals (Mammalia)
Order	Even-toed ungulates (Artiodactyla)
Family	Cloven-hoofed mammals (Bovidae)
Genus	Bison (*Bison*)
Species	There are two species of bison: the American bison (*Bison bison*) and the European bison, or wisent, (*Bison bonasus*)
World Distribution	North America and Central Europe
Habitat	Prairie and woodland
Distinctive physical characteristics	Massive animals with a pronounced shoulder hump; heavy, curved horns that taper to a point; shaggy, woolly coat
Habits	Bison live in herds; they are active mainly by day; they might migrate to find fresh grass
Diet	Grass, other plants, and lichen

Introduction

Many people confuse the bison with the buffalo. The first European explorers in North America called it the buffalo because it looked like pictures of the African and Asian buffaloes. Native Americans have many other names for the bison, such as *tatanka*, *pkocshuke'*, or *yanash*. The word *buffalo* comes from France. In French, the word for "ox" or "beef" is *beouf* (BERF).

Bison are North America's largest native land mammal. They are also a very important part of North American history!

A bison sits and relaxes.

The tallest part of a bison is its muscular hump.

Prairie Heavyweights

A fully grown male American bison, or **bull**, can weigh up to 2,000 pounds (907 kg). That's as much as ten large men! Most of that weight is solid muscle. Imagine a bison thundering past you at a gallop. The ground would shake. Even being close to a big bison standing still might be a little scary. They can be up to 10 feet (3m) long, and their massive humped shoulders are more than 6 feet (2 m) tall.

In fact, the bison is the biggest land animal in North and South America. The bison that live in Canada are a bit smaller than American prairie bison. These Canadian bison are called wood bison because they live mainly in forests.

European Cousins

When most people think of bison, they think of the American species. But there are bison in Europe, too. They have the same ancestors as American bison. Some people think they should all be treated as one species. The European bison is sometimes called the **wisent** (VEE-ZENT). They are smaller than prairie bison and do not live in such large groups. They are forest animals.

There were once wisents all over central and eastern Europe. For hundreds of years people have been hunting European bison and cutting down their forest home. As a result, now the bison live only in a tiny area of protected forest on the borders of Poland and Belarus.

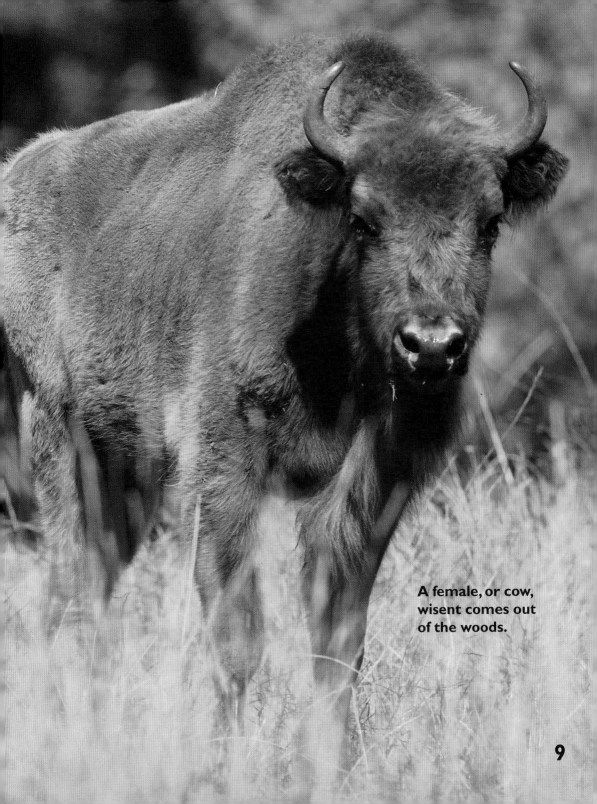

A female, or cow, wisent comes out of the woods.

This painting of a bison from a cave in France is over 13,000 years old.

Family Ties

Bison belong to the same group of animals as cattle, antelope, and sheep. Scientists call all these animals bovids because they belong to a family called the Bovidae (BOH-VUD-AY). The first bovids appeared in Africa about 20 million years ago.

Many tens of thousands of years ago, bison were able to walk from Asia to North America across a narrow strip of land called the Bering land bridge, near present-day Alaska. The ancestors of Native Americans used the same route to get here, too. Then, about 10,000 years ago, the sea rose up and flooded the land bridge. Both bison and people could no longer cross from Asia to North America by land.

Horn Section

Both bulls and female bison, or **cows**, have horns. The horns start growing when the bison are very young. In big bulls the horns can reach 15 inches (38 cm) long. They are thick at the base, which makes them very strong. They curve forward to a sharp pointed tip. Bison use their horns for fighting. Bulls fight each other over cows. Sometimes cows have to fight to defend themselves and their young.

A horn is made of a substance called **keratin**. Keratin is hard, but it is not as brittle as bone. Therefore, a bison rarely breaks its horns. Bison often rub their horns on tree trunks or boulders to polish them and keep the tips sharp.

A bison's horns are made of a tough substance called keratin. Hair and hooves are also made of keratin.

A bison grazes
on grass.

Huge Heads

Bison have a massive head. The skull is very big and heavy. The powerful jaws can grind huge quantities of grass. The weight of the head and the horns means that the bison needs a thick neck and powerful shoulder muscles just to hold its head up. If you look at a bison from the front you'll see its shoulders rising up in a great hump behind its head. The hump is pure muscle.

From a side view the bison almost looks like two different animals stuck together. The front end is very big and powerful. The back end is much smaller and skinnier, like the body of a farm cow.

On the Hoof

Like other hoofed animals, bison have long, slim legs, and special feet. Animals like bears and rats and humans stand on the soles of their feet. But hoofed animals stand on the tips of their toes. Their nails grow very thick and strong to form **hooves**. Bison and their relatives in the cattle and antelope family have just two toes on each foot, each with a hoof. This kind of foot is called a **cloven** hoof, because it looks like a single hoof split in half. The split lets the bison's foot spread a little as it walks or runs. So the foot acts like a shock absorber and gives the bison a better grip on soft or rocky ground.

A bison lies
down and takes
the weight off
its hooves.

A bison enjoys a dust bath in South Dakota.

Coat Care

Bison pay a lot of attention to their coat. That might surprise you because bison often look very dirty, with dust and mud clinging to their coat. But for a bison, a good roll in the dirt is an important part of keeping clean and healthy. That is their way of taking a shower. It helps get rid of loose fur, biting insects, and insects' eggs.

A dust bath also helps get rid of any extra grease in the fur. And just as you might take a nice shower to relax or to wake up, bison really seem to enjoy a good dust or mud bath. Bison use natural dips and hollows in the land for bathing, where the grass is all worn away and the dust or mud collects. These bison bathtubs are called **wallows**.

Staying Together

Bison do not like to be alone, and for good reasons. Even though they weigh as much as ten men and have horns that can pierce through a sheet of metal, bison have to be aware of **predators**. Lone bison are often hunted by packs of wolves. These predators chase their **prey** until the victim is too tired to defend itself. The wolves then attack from the back and the sides, where the bison cannot reach them with its horns.

So for safety, bison prefer to live in groups called **herds**. There are usually between 20 and 60 bison in a herd. Often several herds come together to **graze** or to travel in search of fresh grass. Sometime these "superherds" contain a thousand or more bison.

A herd of bison grazes in Yellowstone National Park, Wyoming.

A bison searches for fresh shoots in the dry grass.

Munching Machines

It's amazing that bison can get so huge by only eating grass. Grass contains a lot of nutrition and energy, but it is difficult to digest. Bison have a complicated digestive system that helps break down the grass. Their digestive system is also very efficient at utilizing all the nutrients from every mouthful of food. Although bison eat mostly grass, when food is scarce they will eat other plants, too. Bison also need to drink water every day.

Chew and Chew Again

Bison spend hours eating grass. Then while they rest, they cough the grass back up one mouthful at a time and give it a long second chew. That is called chewing the cud. Bison teeth are like great knobby grinding stones. These teeth help turn the tough leaves and stems into a pulp, or liquid.

When the pulp is swallowed, it passes into the stomach. There, it is mixed up with tiny single-celled microorganisms called **bacteria**. The bacteria get to work on the grass, helping to break it down. The bacteria turn the tough grass into a sort of sugary soup, which is much easier to digest. The soup passes slowly through the rest of the bison's gut. Every last bit of nutrition is used by the bison's body.

On the Move

Long ago, before the North American prairies were turned into farmland, and before there were towns, railroads, and highways across the Midwest, bison herds could roam wherever they pleased. Herds would wander from one area to another in search of fresh grass, leaving the well-grazed areas to grow. At the end of summer, great herds of bison would often make a journey of up to 200 miles (320 km). The journey ended at wooded areas or sheltered valleys. There the bison would spend winter, protected from the wind and snow.

Over the years, many hundreds of thousands of bison had traveled the same way. They left a clear trail across the land. As humans traveled to the West, they often used these trails. In time the trails became cart tracks, then roads, and sometimes great highways or railroads were built along these bison trails.

A bison rests and chews its cud.

Stampede!

Bison are nervous animals. If they see another bison running, they will run too, in case there is a predator or another danger nearby. Often something simple like a sudden sound will frighten a few bison. Their panic spreads quickly. Soon the whole herd is running as fast as it can. That is a **stampede**.

Stampeding bison will run until they are exhausted. If another animal gets in the way or a bison at the front of the stampede falls, it will be trampled. Because the bison at the back cannot see where they are going, sometimes those at the front are forced to run until they die. Native Americans, who relied on the bison for food, clothing, and shelter, sometimes started stampedes deliberately close to cliffs or rock walls so that a lot of bison would be killed.

Stampeding bison can run as fast as 38 miles per hour (60 km/h).

Two bulls fight
with their horns.

30

Taking Charge

For most of the year, bison herds contain only cows and youngsters up to about three years old. The herds are usually peaceful. All the animals seem to naturally do the same thing at the same time. One of the older females will usually lead the way when the time comes to move to new **pastures** or to stop and rest.

Everything changes in fall, which is the **breeding season**. When the cows in a herd are ready to **mate** they become attractive to bulls. The bulls usually live alone or in all male groups. In the breeding season bulls begin fighting with their horns to try and take charge of the herd. The smaller, younger males are the first to back off. The biggest and strongest bulls may have to fight over and over again to earn the right to stay close to the cows.

Smell and Hearing

Bison have an excellent sense of smell, but they don't only use their nose for picking up scents. They have an extra scent organ in their mouth, called the **Jacobsen's organ**. Cows can only mate for a few days of the year. A bull can tell when that time is near by sniffing the cow and tasting her urine with his Jacobsen's organ.

When a bull takes over a herd of cows, he spends a lot of time rolling in mud and urinating on himself! That makes him smell very strong, and other bison seem to be impressed by the odor. He also spends a lot of time roaring loudly. The roars of the strongest bulls can be heard up to 3 miles (5 km) away. These roars are a good way of showing off to cows and warning other bulls to stay away.

A bison curls its upper lip so scent in the air can reach its Jacobsen's organ.

A bison calf's fur is paler than that of the adults.

New Calves

After a cow has mated with a bull, it takes a little more than nine months until the **calf** is born. Usually there is just one calf, and it is born in summer. Newborn bison can weigh up to 65 pounds (30 kg). That's ten times as much as a human baby.

The first few hours are a dangerous time for a calf and its mother. The pair can become separated from the herd for a short while. But a bison calf is able to stand up and begin walking immediately. At about three hours old, after its first feed of milk, the calf has gained enough strength and control of its legs to be able to run with the herd.

Rough and Tumble

Young bison love to play. As they grow stronger and more confident they spend hours away from their mother, running and leaping, and play-fighting with other youngsters from the herd. They have plenty of energy, which they get from their mother's nutritious milk.

All this playtime is not just about having fun. The exercise is good for the youngsters since it helps their muscles develop and their bones become strong. It also teaches them useful skills such as fighting and how to figure out what another bison is thinking. As the calves get older they also get to know one another's strengths and weaknesses. They might be able to use this information to win battles when they are grown up.

Bison calves in South Dakota play-fight.

A bison keeps watch for signs of danger.

Keeping Watch

As the young bison play, they seem not to have a care in the world. But there is always an adult bison keeping a watchful eye on them. The cows in a herd take turns watching over the youngsters. When not babysitting the calves, the other mothers graze or rest.

Bison use sounds such as grunts and snorts to signal approaching danger. They also use body language to pass on messages. When a bison is worried about something, it raises its tail in the air. Other bison are immediately put on the alert. If they sense a predator, they bunch together in a tight group. That makes it almost impossible for a predator to attack.

Native Americans

For thousands of years before European settlers came to North America, bison and Native Americans lived alongside one another. The Native Americans hunted bison for their meat, hides, and horns. In fact, almost all parts of a bison's body were useful. Without the bison, the people would not have survived. When a bison was killed, the hunters thought of it as a gift from the Great Spirit and would offer their thanks. The bison were respected by the people, and bison spirits appeared in many stories. It was an honor to be named for a bison. The greatest chief of the Sioux tribe was called Tatanka Iyotake, meaning Sitting Bull.

This hand-colored engraving shows Plains Indians hunting bison.

A herd of bison
grazes the prairie
in South Dakota.

The End of an Era

Times changed for the American bison and the Native Americans when people from Europe came to America. Europeans were astounded by the size of the bison herds they saw. Some herds had thousands, even millions, of bison in them. The Europeans had guns. That meant they could hunt bison easily, shooting hundreds in a day. Sometimes the hunters went on foot and shot the bison as they went past. Sometimes they shot from horseback, sometimes even from trains.

By the 1870s, European hunters were killing up to 10,000 bison a day. Sometimes these hunters collected the bison hides and sold them. But they usually left the meat. It wasn't long before the bison were nearly all gone.

Back from the Brink

By the 1880s, when your great, great, great grandparents were young, American bison were almost **extinct**. The great herds that once numbered about 50 million were almost completely gone. In 1887, when people tried to count all the bison on the prairies, they could only find 541.

The bison became a protected species. One man, William Hornaday, began breeding bison in Montana. Gradually the numbers built up again. Some bison were returned to the wild. Today there are about 200,000 bison alive, but most live on private ranches.

This herd of bison lives on Catalina, an island off the coast of California. Bison were first brought to the island in the 1920s.

Wisents are smaller
than American bison
and have shorter hair.

Half a World Away

Things began to improve for the American bison.
But things got even worse for the European bison,
or wisent. One hundred years ago, there were
about 700 wisents left in a forest in Poland. They
were protected until World War I (1914–1918)
started. A few years later all the wild wisents
were gone. Luckily about 50 had been moved
to zoos for protection. The species nearly
became extinct. Today there are about
3,000 wisents left in Europe.

Living History

Today, in North America the bison needs protection. While the number of bison in national parks, reserves, and on private ranches has grown, there are almost no free-roaming herds left.

Bison can be seen in a number of places. Several national parks have bison, including Yellowstone National Park, Theodore Roosevelt National Park in North Dakota, Badlands National Park and Wind Cave National Park—both in South Dakota—and Grand Teton National Park in Wyoming. Bison can also be seen at Tallgrass Prairie Preserve in Oklahoma.

If you don't live near a vast prairie, you can visit bison at the zoo. The National Zoological Park in Washington and the Bronx Zoo in New York both have bison. So do many other zoos.

Words to Know

Bacteria	Tiny living things, just one cell big.
Breeding season	The time of the year when animals come together to produce young.
Bull	A male bison.
Calf	A baby bison.
Cloven	Split in two.
Cows	Female bison.
Extinct	When all of a certain type of animal are dead and gone forever.
Graze	To feed on grass.
Herds	Groups of animals.
Hooves	The hard parts of the feet of a bison, horse, sheep, or other hoofed animal.

Jacobsen's organ	A structure in a bison's mouth that "tastes" scents in the air.
Keratin	A tough material that occurs in horns, hair, and hooves.
Mate	To come together to produce young.
Pastures	An area of grass used for grazing.
Predators	Animals that hunt and eat other animals.
Prey	An animal that is hunted by other animals.
Stampede	A panicked herd of animals running quickly in the same direction.
Wallows	Hollows in the ground where bison roll in dust or mud.
Wisent	Another name for a European bison.

Find Out More

Books

Hinshaw Patent, D. *The Buffalo and the Indians: A Shared Destiny.* New York: Clarion Books, 2006

Winner, C. *Bison.* Our Wild World. Minnetonka, Minnesota: Northward Press, 2001.

Web sites

Bison = American Buffalo
www.enchantedlearning.com/subjects/mammals/bison/Bisoncoloring.shtmlading
Print a picture of a bison to color in.

WWF Northern Great Plains Conservation Results
www.worldwildlife.org/wildplaces/ngp/results.cfm
Information on WWF's bison conservation work.

Index